THE BOOK OF JADE

THE BOOK OF JADE

Park Barnitz

www.General-Books.net

Publication Data:

Title: The Book of Jade
Author: Park Barnitz
Reprinted: 2010, General Books, Memphis, Tennessee, USA
Publication date: 1901
Subjects: American poetry; History / General; Juvenile Nonfiction / Poetry / General; Literary Criticism / Poetry; Poetry / Anthologies; Poetry / American / General
BISAC subject codes: HIS000000, JNF042000, LIT014000, POE000000, POE005010

How We Made This Book for You

We made this book exclusively for you using patented Print on Demand technology.
First we scanned the original rare book using a robot which automatically flipped and photographed each page.
We automated the typing, proof reading and design of this book using Optical Character Recognition (OCR) software on the scanned copy. That let us keep your cost as low as possible.
If a book is very old, worn and the type is faded, this can result in numerous typos or missing text. This is also why our books don't have illustrations; the OCR software can't distinguish between an illustration and a smudge.
We understand how annoying typos, missing text or illustrations, foot notes in the text or an index that doesn't work, can be. That's why we provide a free digital copy of most books exactly as they were originally published. You can also use this PDF edition to read the book on the go. Simply go to our website (www.general-books.net) to check availability. And we provide a free trial membership in our book club so you can get free copies of other editions or related books.
OCR is not a perfect solution but we feel it's more important to make books available for a low price than not at all. So we warn readers on our website and in the descriptions we provide to book sellers that our books don't have illustrations and may have numerous typos or missing text. We also provide excerpts from books to book sellers and on our website so you can preview the quality of the book before buying it.
If you would prefer that we manually type, proof read and design your book so that it's perfect, simply contact us for the cost. Since many of our books only sell one or two copies, we have to split the production costs between those one or two buyers.

Frequently Asked Questions

Why are there so many typos in my paperback?
We created your book using OCR software that includes an automated spell check. Our OCR software is 99 percent accurate if the book is in good condition. Therefore, we try to get several copies of a book to get the best possible accuracy (which is very difficult for rare books more than a hundred years old). However, with up to 3,500 characters per page, even one percent is an annoying number of typos. We would really like to manually proof read and correct the typos. But since many of our books only sell a couple of copies that could add hundreds of dollars to the cover price. And nobody wants to pay that. If you need to see the original text, please check our website for a downloadable copy.

Why is the index and table of contents missing (or not working) from my paperback?
After we re-typeset and designed your book, the page numbers change so the old index and table of contents no longer work. Therefore, we usually remove them. We dislike publishing books without indexes and contents as much as you dislike buying them. But many of our books only sell a couple of copies. So manually creating a new index and table of contents could add more than a hundred dollars to the cover price. And nobody wants to pay that. If you need to see the original index, please check our website for a downloadable copy.

Why are illustrations missing from my paperback?
We created your book using OCR software. Our OCR software can't distinguish between an illustration and a smudge or library stamp so it ignores everything except type. We would really like to manually scan and add the illustrations. But many of our books only sell a couple of copies so that could add more than a hundred dollars to the cover price. And nobody wants to pay that. If you need to see the original illustrations, please check our website for a downloadable copy.

Why is text missing from my paperback?
We created your book using a robot who turned and photographed each page. Our robot is 99 percent accurate. But sometimes two pages stick together. And sometimes a page may even be missing from our copy of the book. We would really like to manually scan each page. But many of our books only sell a couple of copies so that could add more than a hundred dollars to the cover price. And nobody wants to pay that. If you would like to check the original book for the missing text, please check our website for a downloadable copy.

Limit of Liability/Disclaimer of Warranty:
The publisher and author make no representations or warranties with respect to the accuracy or completeness of the book. The advice and strategies in the book may not be suitable for your situation. You should consult with a professional where appropriate. The publisher is not liable for any damages resulting from the book.
Please keep in mind that the book was written long ago; the information is not current. Furthermore, there may be typos, missing text or illustration and explained above.

THE BOOK OF JADE

PRELUDE / am a little tired of all things mortal; I see through half-shut eyelids languorous
   The old monotonous
   Gold sun set slowly through the western portal,
Where I recline upon my deep diwan, In Ispahan.
I am a little weary of the Persian
Girl that I lovd; I am quite tird of love;
And I am weary of
The smoking censers, and the sweet diversion
Of stroking Leilas jasmine-scented hair, I thought so fair.
At last I think I am quite tired of beauty;
Why do the stars shine always in the sky?
I think if I might die,
Something more sweet, less tiring than the duty
Of kissing her, might be; I am tired of myrrh,
And kissing her.
PRELUDE
Khaled, come, come, and slowly move the scented

The Book of Jade. Park Barnitz

Gold narghile away; let the lyres cease.
And now a little peace!
For see, moon-faced Leila hath repented
Of singing Hafis songs melodiously,
And languidly.
Surely all things are vain, and great thanksgiving Is due not; surely all things now are vain;
And all my heart is fain
Of something, something, far too great for living;
Nothing is very sad, nor wonderful,
Nor beautiful.
Well now, since all things are not worth the winning,
Goodbye! With these I have a little playd;
And once, alas, I prayd
That gorgeous, golden sins be mine for sinning;
But now I would not leave my palanquin
For any sin.
And long ago i prov"d in great compassion
For man, that Brahm is not nor ever was;
But now, alas, alas
PRELUDE I would he were, that in the olden fashion
I might laugh once again ere all is said;
But Brahm is dead.
Then with philosophy I bord me duly;
And since I could not slumber all the time,
I, in sweet golden rhyme,
On white papyrus scented with patchouli
Wrote masterpieces starry-beautiful.
The earth was
So beauty wearied me; in order slowly
Love, Jo y, and Victory came unto me;
I kissd them languidly;
rAnd Virtue came, and Duty, stiff and holy;
To these I said–Pray come another day;
And turnd away.
Now since of all I am a little weary,
And since on earth I must a while sojourn,
And since a while must burn
The censer of my long existence dreary,
All things shall walk, that own my mastery, In luxury.
PRELUDE
My Ennui shall in vestments falling lowly,
Stiff, purple, trailing, long, episcopal
Sweep through her palace hall,
Like to a consecrated bishop holy;

My Sin from golden goblets of Byzant
Shall drink absinthe.
And my gold-crowned wanton goddess Pleasure, (My candles are all burning at her shrine)
Shall be made drunk with wine,
And walk unto the velvet-falling measure
Of golden-voiced, solemn-sounding shawms.
No rhyme for shawms.
All they that wait upon me in my glory,
My purple Pride, and my Luxuriousness,
And my Voluptuousness,
Shall show within their faces transitory
Something more subtile than all life can give,
While I shall live.
Ah, all is livd, all eaten, all is drunken!
Soul, is there anything now left for thee
Excepting sanctity?
PRELUDE
Nay, eifn we too have been in virtue sunken, We have been holy priest, we have confessd, Said, Missa Est.
/ have drunk out of heavy goblets golden,
As from some hellish tabernaculum
Cannabis, conium; I know quite all the poisons, all the olden
Sins, all the tenebreux dark secrets hid,
And things forbid.
I have had all things unto mortals given, I all the women, all the passion I,
All the satiety; I have had all the pleasures known in heaven,
Paradisiacal, purpureal,
Exstatical.
With all the sciences I am acquainted,
Alas! I know quite all the languages,
All the philosophies,
Alas! and all the pictures that are painted,
And all the palacd capitals that be
Have wearied me.
PRELUDE
Alas, all art, all knowledge, and all passion I have had: I have heard all the symphonies; I have saild all the seas; I have draind all lifes cup in languid fashion;
And I am come to Persia again,
Land of cocagne.
The Book of Jade Part One
ASHTORETH In thy blue pallid gown that shimmereth
So pale thou standest in the wan moonlight,
Where the gold censer near thy body white
Wraps thee around with its perfumed breath;

So wan thy high tiara glimmereth
Above thy mystical far eyes of light,
Thou seemest some dead goddess of the night,
O starry love, O changeless Ashtoreth.
    Pallid thou standest in thy divinity,
    Like some moon-idol of the buried time,
    Before whose face priests sing in solemn chime.
    So I prostrate before thy deity,
    Unto thy face have solemn praises sung,
    And in my hands a golden censer swung-.

PARFAIT AMOUR

It is not that thy face is fair
    As dying sunsets are,
Nor that thy lovely eyelids wear
    The splendour of a star;
Tis the deep sadness of thine eyes
    Hath my heart captive led, And that within thy soul I prize
    The calmness of the dead.
    O holy love, O fair white face,
    O sweet lost soul of thine!
Thy bosom is an altar-place,
    Thy kisses holy wine;
Sweet incense offerd for my bliss Is thy corrupted breath,
And on thy stained lips I kiss
    The holy lips of Death!

PARFAIT AMOUR

Wherefore because thy heart is all
Filld full of mournfulness, And thy gold head as with a pall
Hung oer with sinfulness; Because thy soul is utterly
Sinful unto the core–Therefore my heart is bound to thee,
Dear love, forevermore!

OPIUM

Naught is more sweet than gently to let dream
The pallid flower of life asleep alway;
Where the dim censer sends up far from day
Unceasingly its still-ascending stream,
    O where the air winds its myrrh-scented steam
About thy naked bodys disarray,
Shall not todays gold to thy shut eyes seem
Born and forgot in the dead ages gray?
    Sunk from lifes mournful loud processional,
    For thee shall not with high uplifted urn
    The Night pour out dreams that awake and say, –We were, O pallid maiden vesperal,
Before the world; we also in our turn
By the vain morning gold scatterd away.

SOMBRE SONNET I love all sombre and autumnal things,
Regal and mournful and funereal,
Things strange and curious and majestical,
Whereto a solemn savor of death clings:
    Coerulian serpents markd with azure rings;
Awful cathedrals where rich shadows fall;
Hoarse symphonies sepulchral as a pall;
Mad crimes adornd with bestial blazonings.
    Therefore I love thee more than aught that dies,
Within whose subtile beauty slumbereth
The twain solemnity of life and death;
    Therefore I sit beside thee far from day
    And look into thy holy eyes alway,
    Thy desolate eyes, thine unillumind eyes.
    LANGUOR
    Although thy face be whiter than the dawn,
Fairer than aught the dawning hath descried,
Hast thou not now, O dear love deified,
Enough of kisses upon thy forehead wan?
    The days and nights, like beads to pray upon,
Pass by before our eyes and not abide,
And so these things shall be till we have died,
Until our bodies to the earth are gone.
    I think how pleasant such a thing must be,
That all thy lovely limbs should fall away,
And drop to nothing in their soft decay.
    Then may thy buried body turn to me,
With new love on thy changed lips like fire,
And kiss me with a kiss that shall not tire.
    ENNUI I sat in tall Gomorrah on a day,
Boring myself with solitude and dreams,
When, like strange priests, with sacerdotal tread,
The seven mortal sinsz in rich array,
    Came in and knelt: one old, and weak, and gray,
One that was shrouded like a person dead,
And one whose robes cast reddish-purple gleams
Upon her scornful face at peace alway.
    They swung before me amschirs of strange gold,
And one most beautiful began to pray,
Dreamily garmented in pallid blue.
    But I said only–I have dreamd of you.
Naught really is; all things are very old,
And very foolish. Please to go away.
    LITANY.
    All the authors that there are bore Me;

All the philosophies bore Me;
All the statues and all the temples bore Me; –All the authors that there are bore Thee;
All the philosophies bore Thee;
All the statues and all the temples bore Thee.
All the women of the earth weary Me;
The fruit of the vine wearieth Me;
All the symphonies weary Me.
–All the women of the earth weary Thee;
The fruit of the vine wearieth Thee;
All the symphonies weary Thee.
Victory and defeat fatigue Me;
Gladness and sorrowing fatigue Me;
Life and death fatigue Me.
–Victory and defeat fatigue Thee;
Gladness and sorrowing fatigue Thee;
Life and death fatigue Thee.

LITANY

The earth and the heavens weary Me;
The sun by day and the moon by night weary Me;
All the great stars of heaven weary Me.
–The earth and the heavens weary Thee;
The sun by day and the moon by night weary Thee;
All the great stars of heaven weary Thee.
The glorious company of the Apostles tireth Me;
The goodly fellowship of the Prophets tireth Me;
The noble army of Martyrs tireth Me.
–The glorious company of the Apostles tireth Thee; The goodly fellowship of the Prophets tireth Thee; The noble army of Martyrs tireth Thee.
All the race of men weary Me;
The Cherubim and the Seraphim weary Me;
Myself wearieth Me.
–All the race of men weary Thee;
The Cherubim and the Seraphim weary Thee;
Thyself wearieth Thee.

HARVARD

On His Twenty-first Year
Tired Muse, put faded roses on thy brow,
Put thy bare arms about the harp, and sing:
–I am a little bord with everything.
Past the closd jalousies the mlengkas go;
They are not beautiful; no Greek they know;
They go about and howl and make a fuss;
I gaze through sad-shapd eyelids languorous,
Far off from Ispahan where roses blow.

Professors sit on lofty stools upcurld,
Through Yankee noses drooling all day long;
I find all these things quite ridiculous.
  Before despisd old age comes over us,
Let us step into the great world ere long.
We shall be very grand in the great world!
  PRIDE
  They come and go, they pass before my soul,
Desire and Love, weak Anguish and Distress,
Shame and Despair: in phantom crowds they press,
Lifes poor processional, Times lowly dole.
  Mournful their voices as slow bells that toll,
Voices of them that curse and do not bless;
Ineffable things wrappd round with loathsomeness,
The deeds that I have done in Fates control.
  They leer and moan, they shriek and threat and lower, Ignoble faces that the sky do mar;
  My changeless soul from her high pride of power
  Looks down unmovd. So the calm evening star
Upon the wallowing peaceless sea looks down,
Set far aloft within the heavens crown.
  SONG OF GOLDEN YOUTH
  Quelle betise! O Muse, no longer lappt in sadness let us lie, Bring the jars of old Falernum, bring the roses ere they die!
  I love laughter, I love kisses, I love Lili, I love love,
But these dingy funeral dirges ennuyer us by-and-by;
Fellows, disinvoltamente, when the lords of life depart,
Lift the wine-cup to your haughty lips, and sing, Good-
bye, goodbye!
We have laughter on our lips, and in our hearts the laughing spring,
  Nothing greatly can afflict us, nor our spirits mortify;
All the laws and regulations under scornful feet we tread,
We laugh loud at all the virtues underneath the shining sky; I have heard, when haughty Tarquin did his horrid deed of sin,
  That Lucretias lily fingers slappd his face vivaciously;
Though of all my life dear Lili make a gay degringolade,
Yet to my ennuis doth Lili sing an endless lullaby;
We are Greeks and we are Tartars, we know all the languages,
  SONG OF GOLDEN YOUTH
  To the girls of Persia, India, China, we know how to sigh;
If the heartless heart of Lili tediously cruel prove,
Go and dance the tarantella with the girls of Hokusai!
In the golden-citied world from Paris unto Tokio
We are quite at home, we saunter languidly through tall
  Shanghai;

Chairete! the shaw of rosy Persia is a gentleman, Charming people in Benares where the Ganges loiters by; Allah akbar! O great world, O golden-towerd cities gay, Into all your gates with laughter and with roses enter I!

Kalliste, your Persian ghazal cease to sing: the sun is low, And the sacred hour of absinthe now is very very nigh.

MAIS MOI JE VIS LA VIE EN ROUGE
Your soul is like a purple flower,
Mary, whose eyes are amethyst,
Whose lips are like red wine when kist, With sweet life and sweet death for dower;
There are who will have none of these,
Who walk in peace all day upright, And in the night pray on their knees–
The pleasures of the life in white.
All clothd with virtues manifold
Are these–their souls are like white snow;
Fair love, around thy heart I know
My heart is bound with chains of gold.
Sweet youths whose life is in the spring,
The water is all wine they drink,
They sorrow not at anything–
The pleasures of the life in pink.
Your gold hairs like an aureole,
Your lips are gold wine bought and sold,
Pure golden kisses bought for gold;
Each breast is like a golden bowl. MAIS MOI JE VIS LA VIE EN ROUGE
These things are for a scorn to those
That read great books both night and day,
That say, Joy dieth as the rose–
The pleasures of the life in gray.
Sweet youths, white ladies, scholars sour,
Rejoice, and hasten on your way;
Mary, whose skin is white as whey,
Your soul is like a purple flower.

LOUANGES DELLE –O Muse of mine that sittest orientally
With a green emerald snake about the waist of thee,
With henna-tinted feet, and almond eyes that dream,
Put down the opium-pipe of jade and ivory,
For she that is most fair is fain to hear thy song:
Awake, O Muse, and sing her praises solemnly,
That to the laughing heart of California
Hath added all the grace of France and Italy;
She who, to put to sleep my pitiless ennuis Is come from distant Paris and from Varsovie;
Athens is in her heart, and Paris in her eyes,
Dear European angel from beyond the sea!

–There is no use to sing; she is not to be sung;
What mortal praise can come unto her glory near?
And she hath quite forgot her natal English tongue;
She is too far, too high, thy languid praise to hear,
Too delicate, too strange, too wicked, too divine,
Too heavenly, too sweet, too bad, too fair, too dear!
Nest-elle pas Ioasis oil tu reves et la gourde
Ou tu humes a longs traits le vin du souvenir f
    HELAS –Why sittest thou, O Muse, in grief enfolden?
–Thou hast me promisd jewels rich and rare
To wear within my hair;
And for my slaves the kings of kingdoms olden;
    And to abide in lofty castles golden,
Because I am most fair.
And lo, I have no sandals for my feet,
And little bread to eat.
    Of that far golden Irem I am dreaming,
Whence for few kisses I did follow thee;
Fair is that spot to see,
    With far-off waving palms and towers gleaming;
Great deserts round that isle of blissful seeming
Lie stretching endlessly.

SONNET

    When I contemplate how my state is low,
And how my pride that had the earth for throne
In this dark city sitteth all alone,
My heart is fain for death to end its woe;
    Then when I think how all the great below
Had only sorrow and grief through all their days,
I, that with these shall some time stand in place,
My fortune like their bitter fortune know.
    Among whom also holy Baudelaire,
Though unto him the loftiest lot was given
To hear the blessed muses sing in heaven,
    Past his few days in anguish and despair;
Yet did he not bow down his mournful head
Until Peace found him in his glory dead.
    So thou in this low lair,
      Although in sorrow and grief thou dost remain,
      Though of all things whereof thy soul was fain
      Remaineth only pain,
      Yet be not thou, O soul, disconsolate:
      Forget not thou thy far-exalted state.

SONNET

Be not cast down my heart, and be not sad,
That thou like common men must sorrow know;
Not only they that live and die below,
But evn the gods thy supreme sorrow had;
　　Not unto Tammuz was this fortune given,
Not to know grief; whom starry Ashtoreth
Sought through the seven-gated realm of death,
Far from the great moon and the stars of heaven.
　　Osiris also could not but to die;
　　He reigneth king among the perisht dead;
　　And Christ, when his long grief was finished,
Hid his great glory in the lowly ground. All these had sorrow, that were great and high; These also were august, these also crownd.

RONDEAU

　　As shadows pass, in the misty night,
Over the wan and moonlit grass,
　　So passeth our glory out of sight,
As shadows pass.
　　A little darkness, a little light,
　　Sorrow and gladness, a weary mass, Glimmer and falter and pass in blight.
　　So all our life, in waning flight,
　　Fadeth and faltereth, alas; Passeth our sorrow and our delight,
　　As shadows pass.

AUTUMN SONG

　　Weep, far autumnal skies,
Shrouded in misty air;
　　Weep, for thy solemn dearth,
And for thy chill despair,
Earth.
　　O stricken forest-trees,
　　Dead leaves that falter down Solemnly to your sleep,
　　Golden, and red, and brown,
Weep.

BALLAD

　　The lady rode neath the strange skys pall
Through the leafy woods funereal,
And all the length of her moonlit way
Was wanly white as the light of day;
Solemnly robd she rode along,
Unmindful of their droning throng
That throngd her shadowy path, alas,
As though to see her funeral pass;
So through the mournful forest slow
Her palfreys silken feet did go,
Bearing her solemnly like a god

Over the shadow-haunted sod;
She laught to see the dead desire
That even now her life should tire,
She laught to think that to the earth
They calld her that was full of mirth,
And though before her horses head
Throngd the wan legions of the dead
Wanly attempting to stop her way,
She halted not for their legions gray,
But rode through the midnights mystic noon
Under the far gaze of the moon.

BALLAD

Then out from the dying woods at last
Into the moonlit plain she passt;
The misty stars were almost dead
Sunk in the heavens overhead,
While low down in the solemn skies
The white moon wand as one that dies.
Solemnly through the misty air
She rode with gold gems in her hair;
Bright were her holy eyes divine,
And red her lips as the red red wine.
At last in the unceasing night
Down from her palfrey she doth alight
By the strange murmuring of the sea;
She climbs the tall stair fearlessly,
And cometh at last to her chamber high
Beneath the wide face of the sky.
At last her journey being done,
She hath her golden stays undone,
And being a little wearied,
Hath laid her naked on her bed,
Thinking to slumber like the dead.

CHANGELESSNESS

When Death shall touch thy body beautiful,
And thou that art of all the earth most fair
Shalt close thine eyes upon the shining air,
An unadorned gold urn to make full;
    When that thou liest quietly inurnd In the dark bosom of the earth divine,
    Being turned unto a heap of ashes fine,
    For love of whose white face all men have burnd;
    Then in the earth, O beautiful white love,
Thy beauty shall not wholly end and cease,
When that thou art gone to endless peace;

Though all things beneath the sky above
Fade away, it knoweth not to die,
But abideth changeless endlessly.

MADONNA

Anguish and Mourning are as gold to her;
She weareth Pain upon her as a gem,
And on her head Grief like a diadem;
And as with frankincense and tropic myrrh

Her face is fragrant made with utter Woe;
And on her purple gorgeous garments hem
Madness and Death and all the ways of them
Emblazoned in strange carousal show.

Within her delicate face are all things met, And all the sad years and the dolorous days Are but as jewels round her forehead set,

Add but a little glory to her face,
A little languor to her half-closd eyes,
That smile so strangely under the far skies.

POPPY SONG

O poppy-buds, that in the golden air Wave heavy hanging censers of delight, Give me an anodyne for my despair;

O crimson poppy-blooms, O golden blight, O careless drunken heavy poppy-flowers, Make that the day for me be as the night.

Give me to lie down in your drowsy bowers, That having breathed of your rich perfume, My soul may have all-rest through all the hours;

So shall I lie within my little room, While the poor tyrants of the world go by, Restfully shrouded in your velvet gloom,

Beneath the wide face of the cloudless sky.

–Even so, when thou shalt eat of us, Even so, thy life shall be a sleep, Empty of all things fierce and piteous;

Even as a sailor on the tossing deep Hears vaguely the vain tumult on the shore, Shouts of the fighters, songs of them that reap.

Life is all vanity, a loathed sore, A scatterd dust, a vain and soiled heap.–Thou shalt have golden rest forevermore.

POPPY SONG

O poppy-flowers, golden, sleepy, sweet, O yellow tawny fading blooms of gold, Give unto me your holy fruit to eat;

Make me forget all things above the mould; Make me forget that dolorous vow that sears, Not to be lesser than the great of old;

Make me forget the heavy old dead years, And all that lives from out the writhing past, Old struggles, dead ambitions, buried tears;

And that white face that I shall see the last.

–Sweet is forget fulness, most sweet to lie, Sunken from sorrow, in our pleasant vale, Where but the sun shines, and the clouds go by;

Even as to them that through deep waters sail The toiling shore fades and becomes a sky, And evermore behind the billows fail.

Sweet to forget the death-like things that were, Green pastures where the clouds sail by on high, Dead sundawns over pathless prairies fair,

And suns long sunk beneath the wall of the sky.

Under the sun my spirit lies alone, Drunken with slumber and mild exstasy. POPPY SONG

Sleep, sweet sleep, long unto mine eyes unknown. Drops on me as ripe fruit drops from a tree; My dim eyes see the valley poppy-strown;

The clouds fade and the gold sun over me, And the worlds murmur sounds within my lair Like the far tossing of some infinite sea;

Within the heavy slumber-laden air
All fades, all fades, and grows afar afar,
Leaving my soul alone, empty of care,
Even as happy long-dead bodies are.
Even so I slumber in my tireless close,
While the whole world fades like a fading star,
Dies like the perfume of a dying rose.
CONSOLATION
Among all sorrows that my heart hath known,
Among all sorrows that my spirit keep
Forever buried neath their mountains steep,
Standeth one consolation, one alone.
I know that earth shall be for death a throne,
And evermore within their burials deep
The banded nations of the earth shall sleep,
Sunken in sepulchres of sculpturd stone.
Then all the world shall be a quietness:
Dead women beautiful with their delights;
All they that had such striving and distress,
And endless weariness in all the lands,
White faces, eager heart-strings, soiled hands;
And peace shall hold the valleys and the heights.
LIEBES-TOD
Thy splendour-lighted face before mine eyes
Shines like a naming sunset evermore;
Thee only I behold on the earths floor,
Thee only I behold within the skies;
Thy coming on is like a conqueror,
Before thy footsteps the worlds glory dies,
Within mine ears thy voice doth ever rise
Like a loud ocean beating on the shore.
Thou art made kindred with eternity,
Daughter of glory, daughter of consolations;
Thy face is set above the constellations;

Of Death! O love! be I made one with thee,
That on thy holy lips and in thy love
The world may perish and the light thereof!
   LIEBES-TOD
II
   Lo, now my life is gone unto eclipse
Upon thy perilous bosom; lo, I die,
Faint with the utter whole of exstasy,
With unassuaged lips against thy lips,
   That can give no more joy; lo, at the place
Of utter joy, lo, at joys far-off throne,
Which none shall reach, with eyes now weary grown,
I lie slain at its utmost golden base.
   Yea, we have calld the white stars to behold
Our pale and fainting faces sick with joy; 0 regal lips that shall deaths sting destroy, I have suckd. bare lifes cup upon thy breath! Kiss me to death! Lo, now our lips are cold, Wilt thou not bring new joy, O Death, O Death?
   EVENING SONG
   Lo, all the passionate pale evening I lay between the breasts of my beloved,
   Among the lilies, in the lily garden.
   The sky was pale, and all the sunset faded,
   And all the stars I saw not in the heaven,
   Because the glory of her face above me I saw alone, wrapt in a dream of slumber;
   And lo, she was more fair than all the lilies,
   Among the lilies, in the lily garden.
   And all her hair was golden chains to bind me,
   And all her mouth was crimson fire to burn me,
   And all the world became as wind before me,
   But as the wind before her face that passes,
   Among the lilies, in the lily garden.
   And lo, her face was fairer than the stars are,
   And lo, her breasts were whiter than the moon is,
   Whiter than the moon, and tippd with crimson coral.
   And low she bowd her body, low before me,
   And gave me of her joy unto fulfilling:
   She bowd her head whereto the stars do homage,
   Before whose face the years wax dim and fading,
   EVENING SONG
   Before whose eyes the ages pass and vanish;
Bowd her low down before me like a lily,
Among the lilies, in the lily garden.
And now at last I care not if the morning
Come at all, or the pale stars have setting,
Nay I care not if the whole world perish,
Perish and die, or if the white stars falter,

Nay I care not if the night forever
Hold me by her, and all things have ceasing;
Yea, because her lips are more than roses,
Yea, because her breasts are more than Heaven,
Yea, because her face is more than God is,
Among the lilies, in the lily garden.

SONG OF THE STARS IN PRAISE OF HER

O starry light of the dim universe!
The night adoreth thee, the planets high
That reign far off within the desert sky
Praise thee as with the sound of dulcimers,
And all the temples of the night rehearse
Thy solemn glory everlastingly!

    O thou for whom the moons pale-lighted star
    And all the planets and the milky gleam,
    But as a little of thy praising seem,
    And the great lights that swim through heaven afar
    But the reflection of thy glory are;
    Thou only art; these are but shine and dream;
    Thou art that light that doth the stars illume,
Thou art the glimmer of the moon divine;
All these are but the garment that is thine;
Thou art the wonder and the glow, the bloom,
Thou art the lonely lamp in nights great gloom,
Thou art the skyey light, the starry shine.

SONG OF THE STARS IN PRAISE OF HER

Starlight is but the glory of thy face,
The shimmer of the silver planets pale Is but the dim effulgence of thy veil;
And the great passing of the nights and days Is all but as the perfume of thy praise.
O Holy, Holy, Holy, hail, O hail!

AUBADE

The lady awoke before the cold gray dawn,
And had no joy thereof;
–What joy is mine of all the joy of love,
When love is gone?

    Lo, all the air is strange unto mine eyes,
Lo, all the stars are dead;
Only the moon appeareth overhead
As one that dies.

    Lo, all the garden lieth desolate,
And very strange to see,
Wherein, the roses and the grass for me
Blossomd of late.

    O rose-garden wherein my roses grew,
O odorous dim ways,

Why are ye strange to me as perishd days,
And cold with dew?

AUBADE

Through the wide window creeps the cold sweet air,
Faint with sweet rose-perfume, It stealeth oer my body in the gloom,
And oer my hair.
Surely I have drunk full of loves delight,
But now my lips are cold,
While the pale day in silence doth behold
The dying night.

REMEMBER

Remember, ye whom the skies delight,
Whose faces flame with the falling sun, That after sunset cometh the night, That sorrow followeth all delight,
When love, and lover, and lovd are one.
O ye whose days are as sands that run,
One house there is unknown of delight, One garden is there belovd of none, One place there is unseen of the sun, Remember, ye whom the skies delight.

SONG

She hath livd the life of a rose,
She that was fair,
Blown on by the summer air, Grown tall in a golden close.
An ending is set to delight;
Now thou art as grass,
As the leaves, as the blossoms that pass, Made pale at the touch of the night.

SONG

Cometh a day and a night,
When the lamps of life burn dim, When peace is securd for delight,
And poppies for the red-rose flower;
When the lamps of life burn dim, Cometh a day and a night,
A day and a night and an hour.
Cometh the end of the years,
When the cheeks have the lilies bloom, When slumber is given for tears,
And the breasts to the worm belong;
When the cheeks have the lilies bloom, Cometh the end of the years,
As silence after the song.
Cometh a day and a night
For him to whom all is thrown, Whose own is the bosom white,
Whose own are the lips of gold;
For him to whom all is thrown, Cometh a day and a night,
To have and to own and to hold.

CONSTANCY

Surely thy face, love, is a little pale,
And somewhat wan thy lips that were so red,

And though my kisses might raise up the dead,
To waken thy deep sleep they naught avail.
  Before thy stillness some poor men might quail,
But I shall not desert thy holy bed,
Although thy passionate lips have no word said,
And thine adored breasts are cold like hail.
  Thou art gone down to Death, thou art gone down,
And the dead things shall nestle in thy hair,
And the dust shall profane thy golden crown,
  And the worms shall consume thy perfect face;
Even so: but Death shall bring thee no disgrace,
And to the stars I cry, Thou art most fair!
  REQUIEM
  White-rose perfume
  Go with thee on thy way
  Unto thy shaded tomb;
  Low music fall
  Lightly as autumn leaves
  About thy solemn pall;
  Faint incense rise
  From many a censer swung
  Above thy closed eyes;
  And the sounds of them that pray
  Make thy low bier an holy thing to be,
  That all the beauty underneath the sun
  Carries unto the clay.
  Odour of musk and roses
Make sweet thy crimson lips
Whereon my soul hath gone to deep eclipse;
Poppies and violets scent
Be for thy burial lent
    And every flower that sweetest smell discloses. REQUIEM
    Upon thy breast,
    Before which all my spirit hath bowd down,
    White lilies rest;
    And for a crown upon thy mortal head
    Be poppies red.
    And for eternal peace
    Be poppies strown upon thy holy eyes,
    Till also these shall cease
    Turning to that which man is when he dies.
    And poppies on thine unassuaged mouth
    Be strown, until death shall be done with thee,
    Until the white worms shall be one with thee.
    AUTUMN BURIAL

The moon shone full that night,
And filld with misty light
The solemn clouds hung white
    Above her pall;
Waiting the golden dawn
The silent woods stood wan,
While through their aisles movd on
    Her funeral.
    Palely their torches flare,
While robd in white they bear
Her corpse that was most fair
    Of them that die,
By sleeping forests tall
And woods funereal
Through the decaying fall
    Beneath the sky.
    The orbed moon looks down
Upon her golden crown,
From out the forest brown
The wood-things stare;

AUTUMN BURIAL

    The holy stars behold
Her woven hair of gold,
And slumbering and cold
Her bosom bare.
    The moon shines full oerhead,
And they with bowed head
About her body dead In silence stand; There where no foot hath trod They bury her with sod Alone with only God In all the land.
    Tall forests stand around
About her grassy mound
And over all the ground
    Lie shadows hoar.
She neath the passing moon
Sees not the shadows strewn
Sunk in her golden swoon
    Forevermore.

SONNET OF BURIAL

    Now that the earth thy buried corpse doth hold,
Now that thy soul that hath so much desired,
Is gone down to the places of the tired,
Far from the dawning and the star-light cold;
    Thine eyes shall not again the sun behold;
Now shall thy body that all men hath fired

Have ceasing, and thy grave shall be admired,
That doth the fairest thing o the earth enfold.
    Now that thine ashes are all buried,
    And thou art gone to slumber with the blessed,
    Thy buried body shall be no more distressed;
    Being now numberd with the placid dead,
    Thine eyes forever more have ceasd from weeping,
    Forevermore thy spirit shall have sleeping.

NOCTURNE

    Lo, how the moon, beloved,
Far in the heavens gleaming,
Over the ocean dreaming
Her pallid light doth throw;
    Lo, where the endless ocean,
Where softly the night wind bloweth,
Into the darkness floweth,
Thither at last I go.
    Listen, how sweet the ocean
Unto our spirits sigheth,
And lo, where our pinnace lieth
Awaiting, with sails unfurld;
    Come thou with me, beloved,
Come thou with heart unquailing,
There where no ships come sailing,
Out of the dreary world.

NOCTURNE

    Come thou with me, beloved,
Out of the world and its seeming,
Where all things are only dreaming,
And shadows all we know;
    The heart hath not found its longing
Here, nor shall find it ever;
Behold of my lifes endeavour
Remaineth only woe.
    Behold, my desire, my anguish,
Trouble and toil surpassing,
Are all but as shadows passing,
Shadows the fame thereof;
    Here, where the heart attaineth
Not, what the heart desireth,
Where beauty too early tireth,
And kisses mean not love.
    Here where what man hath desired,
He shall not find forever,

But ever and only ever
Unending vanity;
    NOCTURNE
    Not in this world, beloved,
My only longing hideth,
But in farther lands abideth
And over a wider sea.
    There, when the spring shall blossom,
There, when the winter is vanisht,
My spirit that long was banisht
Shall come to its home, though late;
    There in mine olden kingdom,
Where nothing is transitory,
I in exceeding glory
Shall hold mine ancient state.
    Here let us leave our anguish,
Here at the hour of leaving,
Leave we our woe and grieving
Like garments long outworn;
    Leave we our mortal sorrow,
Our longing and our repenting,
The anguish and the lamenting
That made our hearts to mourn.
    NOCTURNE
    Others may weep and anguish,
Others may talk of laughter,
And ever a little after
Sorrow is theirs the more;
    But we two have done with laughter
And sadness that hath no reason,
We two in the springtime season
Push out from the weary shore.
    Past are the storms of winter,
Past is the rainy weather,
Past are the snows, together
With sadness and sorrowing;
    Past are the rains, beloved,
    Past is the time of weeping,
    And lo, oer the green earth sleeping,
    Laugheth the world-wide Spring!
    Come thou with me, beloved,
O let us now be starting!
All things, at the hour of parting,
Shall be made new for thee;
    NOCTURNE

Listen, how sweet the ocean
Unto our spirits calleth;
Softly the starlight falleth
Over the dreaming sea.
  Fadeth the land, beloved,
That long hath our spirits tired,
Before us lies that desired
Far country, strange and new;
  Far off lies that dreamd-of country
Eternally fair and blessed
Eternally undistressed,
Far over the ocean blue.
  Knowst thou the land, beloved?
Year-long with gentle motion
There the unending ocean
Batheth the tropic shore;
  There never storms blow loudly,
There never wet rain falleth,
There never loud wind calleth,
Nor stormy waters roar.
  NOCTURNE
  Fairer the stars that lighten
There, than to us is given,
There in a fairer heaven
Shineth a larger moon;
  Fair stand the castles golden
There, and oer stranger flowers
There through the long long hours
The wandering breezes swoon.
  There in that land, beloved,
Is never a sound of living,
Never is heard thanksgiving
There, nor the noise of moan;
  There naught is heard of sorrow,
And nothing is there begotten;
There, with all life forgotten,
We two shall come alone.
  There, O my one beloved,
Through twilight never-closing,
We two shall sit reposing,
Forever, thou with me;
  NOCTURNE
  There neath the stars eternal,
We two shall sit, we only,

While from the heavens, lonely,
The moon sinks in the sea.

The Book of Jade Part Two

MAD SONNET

Lo, in the night I cry out, in the night,
God! and my voice shall howl into the sky!
I am weary of seeing shapeless things that fly,
And flap into my face in their vile flight; I am weary of dead things that crowd into my sight,
I am weary of hearing horrible corpses that cry,
God! I am weary of that lidless Eye
That comes and stares at me, O God of light!
    All, all the world is become a dead blur,
    God! God! and I, stricken with hideous blight,
    Crouch in the black corners, and I dare not stir.
    I am aweary of my evil plight.
    If thou art not a dead corpse in thy sky,
    Send thou down Death into my loathed sty!

THE HOUSE OF YOUTH

    Far in the melancholy hills it stands,
    Far off; and through the vista of the years,
Down which my soul its helpless journey steers,
It flames a fire to lighten all the lands,
A fire that burns me and a flame that brands
Me, whose dead days pass slow as heavy tears.

    The road my footsteps tread is dim and still,
There darkness abides and silence endlessly,
And the low way mine eyes can scarcely see;
And yet the light and sound from that far hill
Like the skys fire my weary pathway fill,
So that it seems a place of life to be.

    The world is but a background for it there,
There where it stands, loud like a beaten lyre,
And flames blood-red like some vast funeral-pyre,
    Whereat my heart to fail doth not forbear;
    Of all the things that have been made soeer
Only the House remains, a quenchless fire.

THE HOUSE OF YOUTH

    Ah God, that this thing were not in the world–
The hateful House that flames with light and song
And weary singing all the ages long;
Ah that evn this might in the dust be hurld,
And crushd and slain, even as my heart, where curld
The kindly armies of the worm do throng.

Yea, surely I have seen it long ago,
Far sunken in the weary dust of time;
Yea surely even that stair so hard to climb I climbd, and strode its hallways to and fro;
The which were bright with many lamps aglow,
And loud with choristers in ceaseless chime.

DE PROFUNDIS

Out of the grave, O God, I call to thee,
Be thou not deaf unto my dolorous cry;
My soul is fallen down into the sty,
And the dead things are crawling over me; 0 thou my God, give me the worm to flee,
Out from the pits depths I would rise on high.

Again am I fallen down into the grave,
My soul is sunken in the place of slime,
I am too weak its loathed walls to climb,
Thou, only thou, O God, art strong to save;
Lo, in mine eyes the worms have made their cave, And squatting toads oppress me all the time.

Yea, from this pit I have crawld out before; With groans and cries and many a dolorous fall, I have climbed up its impregnable wall; 1 shall not rise now from its slimy floor; O God, hear thou my lamentable call,
Or from the grave I come not evermore.

DE PROFUNDIS I am become a housing for the toad;
All things are fled wherein I took delight; There is no joy here, and there is no light; 0 God, O God, I have reapd what I sowd; 1 am become a dead thing in the night,
And in my heart the worms have their abode.

Lo, from my body all my might is fled,
And all the light is gone out of mine eyes;
Mine ears hear only lamentable cries,
And eyeless things stand round about my head; I am made as a man that slowly dies;
I am made as a man already dead.

PRAYER IN TIME OF PLAGUE

Holy Pestilence, holy Pestilence, gird thee with might, Holy Pestilence, come thou upon them, come thou at night,

Holy Pestilence, put on thy mantle, put on thy crown, Holy Pestilence, come on the cities, come and strike down, Holy Pestilence, let them all perish, touchd with thy breath,

Holy Pestilence, let them grow rotten, moulding in death, Holy Pestilence, put on thy garments, a crown on thy head,

Holy Pestilence, let all the nations fall at thy tread, Holy Pestilence, let them all perish, let them be dead.

Holy Pestilence, then shall the cities sink with thy might, Holy Pestilence, they shall lie desert, plague-struck at night, Holy Pestilence, then shall the rulers, crownd with a crown,

PRAYER

Holy Pestilence, feeling them stricken, reel and fall down, Holy Pestilence, then shall the nations faint with thy breath, Holy Pestilence, then shall the valleys be coverd with death,

Holy Pestilence, peasant with ruler, body with head, Holy Pestilence, all shall be stricken under thy tread, Holy Pestilence, all shall be rotten, all shall be dead.

SESTETTES

Thou shalt rejoice for woe:
The pallid goblet old,
That holds thy lifes dull wine,
Is made thereby divine;
Staind with a purpler glow,
And wrought in stranger gold.

II

From the suckd lees of pain,
We have won joy again:
Death shall thee not distress:
That sleepy bitterness
To thy kist lips shall be
The supreme exstasy.

Ill

Put ashes on your golden body bare,
Puissant as musk, bitter-sweet as to die,
Ashes upon your arms that grow not old,
And on your unassuaged lips of gold:
So we will wanton in loves sepulchre,
And mock the face of Death with blasphemy.

SESTETTES

IV I love you more than Death: your mournful head,
Your shrouding hair, and your unfathomd eyes,
And your white body beautiful, alas,
Priestess and victim in loves holy mass.
Your flesh that loves, and loving ever dies.
I could not love you more if you were dead.

Death is death; the little host that squirms,
The smell, the dark, the coffin closd, and I
So soft, so soft; no movement, and no breath;
No ears, no nose, no eyeballs; Death is Death;
The sepulchre, no sight, no sound, no cry,
And always; Death is Death; the worms! the worms!

Not for your evil is my spirit sad– I mourn because you are not really bad;
Because your beautys perfect cruelty Is ever marrd with pity and distress,
And you still show within your wickedness
The poor stale weakness of humanity.

 VII I am as one that thirsteth for all things,
As one that holdeth to his lips the cup,
 SESTETTES
 With lowerd eyes searching the wines dull flame.
No thing may I refuse among all things,
Till, having draind unto its dregs the cup,
I may return into the astral flame.
 VIII
 Heart, we have wholly draind the cup of sadness,
 And found in sadness no reality;
 Now from the night of sadness let us go.
 Henceforward let us drain the cup of gladness,
 And find in gladness no reality;
 From sadness then and gladness let us go.
 SONNET OF THE INSTRUMENTS OF DEATH
 Adorned daggers, ruby-hilted swords;
Huge mortal serpents in gold volumes rolld;
All-holy poisons in wrought cups of gold;
Unfailing crucifixes of strong cords;
 Mortal baptismal waters without fords,
Wherein lie deaths communicants untold–
Which of these instruments blessed and old,
Is meetest for lifes purple-robed lords?
 Ye that commune in deaths ciborium,
 Of all the vessels in his sacristy
 Which will ye choose to make of you a clod–
 Sharp swords, bright lightnings, orient opium?–
All these, brave souls, are of one sanctity;
All ways are good whereby ye pass to God.
 TRUTH It is not that I have not sought thy face
Ceaselessly through the worlds eternal lie,
More than all things and throughout every place,
Which having seen I were content to die.
 But I have sought thee and I have not found;
Wherefore my soul is banishd from delight,
And sitteth joyless as a madman bound
Seeing vain visions in the loathed night.
 I know not even that I do not know,
 But all things waver before me to and fro;
 As one half head that would be dead I lie.
 And thou, Death, if thy face be really fair,
I know not, or but renewal of vanity;
Wherefore mine eyes have seen the last despair.
 HEGEL

Because my hope is dead, my heart a stone,
I read the words that Hegel once did write–
An idiot gibbering in the dark alone–
Till on my heart and vision fell the night.

MONOTONY

A dead corpse full of wormy questionings,
Beneath the open sky my soul lies dead,
Shameless and rotten and unburied,
For whom eternity no difference brings.

Only the wind my loathed incense flings
Afar afar; only above my head
Day passes, night returns when day is fled,
Unchangeable return of changeless things.

Unto the dead all things bring only pain,
And evermore my perishd heart is woe
For the vile worms that gnaw it lying low;

While the dead days, like to an endless chain,
Pass ever oer my body cruelly slow,
And evermore with pain return again.

SEPULTURE

My heart is but a tomb, where vain and cold
My dead hopes lie: encoffind there my Pride
Lies dead, and my Lifes Gladness crucified,
And there my Morning Joy long turnd to mould;

And there like once-lovd corpses dead and old
My Victory that long long since hath died,
And all my Hopes lie shrouded side by side,
For whom no eyes have wept, no dirges tolld.

And there insensate on the darkend floor
Despair a maniac still doth howl and scream,
Among all these long dead alive alone;

Among these things I sit upon a throne, In endless contemplation evermore;
Nor these suffice to break my iron dream.

MISERRIMUS
In the last hopeless depth of hells dark tomb
Wherein I sit for aye with bowed head
In anguish and great sorrow buried
Where never sun the blackness doth illume, I saw pass by me through the bitter gloom
All them whom life with deepest grief hath fed,
Whom also here among the hopeless dead
Through hell pursueth maniac, gnashing doom.

Me there forever crusht to hopeless stone
They passt by, all the damnd; they shall not know
Through all eternity but only woe,
Now hear no sound but sound of them that groan.

And unto me that sat than these more low,
These seemd like happy gods that heaven own;
They past away; and there in hell alone
My heart took up again its ancient woe.

SCORN

Dead am I, and ye triumph oer me dead,
Ye that within mine eyes have found your home,
Ye that are soft and blind and white like foam,
Ye that have made of me your meat and bread.

Unto the worms I am abandoned;
Over my flesh their loathed cohorts roam;
Upon my heart whereto their hosts have clomb
Their hungry lips shall evermore be fed.

Here am I but a dead corpse in a tomb;
I shall not out from my accursd abode,
Inhabited by the dull worm and the toad;

Ye vile sojourners in my rotten room,
Torment me with your everlasting goad!
I scorn you till the end shall come of doom.

THE GRAVE

The loathed worms are crawling over me
All the dead hours; about my buried head
Their soft intolerable mouths are gathered,
   And in my dead eyes that have ceasd to see.
   I am full of worms and rotten utterly,
      Dead, dead, dead, dead, dead, dead, dead, dead, dead, dead.
      The lifeless earth lies close against mine eyes; I know that I have rotted long ago;
   My limbs are made one with the worms I know
Where all my head and body putrifies.
So in the earth my coffind ordure lies
   Within my loathed shambles strait and low.
   There is no thing now where my face hath been,
   And all my flesh lies soft upon the floor;
   Unto my heart the worms have found a door,
And all my body is to the worms akin;
They long time since their feasting did begin,
   And they shall part not from me evermore.

THE GRAVE

Here lie I stretchd out through the rotting years,
And I am surely weary of the grave,
And I have sometimes thought that I might rave,
   And my two perishd eyes almost shed tears.
   There is no one that sees and none that hears;
I shall not out from my corrupted cave.

Here now forever with the lustful worms
I lie within my putrid sunken sty,
And through eternity my soul shall die.
  O thou toward whom all my dead spirit squirms!
  Forevermore I love thee through all terms
Until the dead stars rot in the black sky.

MUMMY

  Thou art at last made perfect; from the estate
Of mushy life Death hath thee petrified.
The soft the flowing and the putrified
That made thee up, is by that artist great
  Now crystallizd unto a changeless state.
  That thing thou walkedst, nosd and eard and eyed,
  Eternally severely doth abide,
  Sunk from the bands of them that drank and ate.
  Green mummies walk above thy walled gloom,
  Unripend mummies; they intemperate
  Seek in lifes beauty their high-crowned doom In vain. But thee no passion doth illume
Stiff in the musked darkness of the tomb
Hard in stiff bands of red and nacarat.

SEPULCHRAL LIFE

  Lo, all the world as some vast corpse long dead,
Fadeth and perisheth and doth decay,
Even as a corpse, in whose unhonord clay
The worms have long the inmost secrets read;
  Even as a corpse, upon whose lowly head
The sun beats, and the holy rain doth play;
Even as a corpse, whereof the people say,
–We would that these dead bones were buried.
  Even so: and in the earths vast sepulchre
  Our fainting souls their doubtful footsteps bear,
  Dreaming of that which no dead men may see;
  And in our passage to the second death,
  We whisper strange names with our pesty breath,
  Of Love, and Honour, and great Victory.

CORPSE

  A dead corpse crowned with a crown of gold
Sits thrond beneath the skys gigantic pall;
Gold garments from its rotted shoulders fall,
And regal purple robes funereal.
  Before its face a vast processional
Goes by with offerings for its great knees cold;
Its soft hand doth a golden sceptre hold;
And in its flesh lie sleeping worms uprolld.

They that pass ceaseless by see not at all;
They know not that beneath its garments fold
Is but a corpse, rotted, and dead, and tall.

He is accurst that sees it dead and old;
He is accurst that sees: the white worms call
For him: for him have funeral dirges tolld.

MANKIND

They do not know that they are wholly dead,
Nor that their bodies are to the worm given oer;
They pass beneath the sky forevermore;
With their dead flesh the earth is cumbered.

Each day they drink of wine and eat of bread,
And do the things that they have done before;
And yet their hearts are rotten to the core,
And from their eyes the light of life is fled.

Surely the sun is weary of their breath;
They have no ears, and they are dumb and blind;
Long time their bodies hunger for the grave.

How long, O God, shall these dead corpses rave?
When shall the earth be clean of humankind?
When shall the sky cease to behold this death?

THE DEFILERS

O endless idiocy of humankind!
O blatant dead that howl and scream and roar!
O strange dead things the worms have gambled for!
O dull and senseless, foolish, mad and blind!

How long now shall your scent defile the wind?
How long shall you make vile the earths wide floor?
How long, how long, O waiting ages hoar,
Shall the white dawn their gaping faces find?

O vile and simple, blind of heart and mind,
When shall your last wave roll forevermore
Back from the sick and long-defiled shore?

When shall the grave the last dead carcass bind?
O shameless humankind! O dead! O dead!
When shall your rottenness be buried?

THE GROTESQUES

I saw a dead corpse lying in a tomb,
Long buried and rotten to the core;
Behold this corpse shall know not evermore
Aught that may be outside its wormy room; It lies uncoverd in the pesty gloom,
Eyeless and earless, on the enamel-floor,
While in its nameless corpse the wormlets hoar
Make in its suppurated brain their room.

And in that charnel that no lights illume, It shriekd of things that lay outside its door;

And while the still worms through its soft heart bore, It lay and reasond of the ways of doom,
    And in its head thoughts movd as in a womb;
    And in its heart the worms lie evermore.
207512
THE GROTESQUES
    I saw a dead corpse in a haughty car,
Whom in a high tomb phantom horses bore,
Aye to and fro upon the scatterd floor;
His dead eyes stard as though they lookd afar,
    His gold wheels myriad perishd souls did mar,
While through his flesh the ravenous wormlets tore;
He in whose eyes the worm was conqueror,
Held his high head unmoved like a star.
    And as with loud sound and reverberant jar,
And as with splash of crusht flesh and dull roar,
The death-car thunderd past the tomb-walls hoar,
    Within those dead dominions the dead tsar
Receivd his plaudits where dead bodies are;
And in his heart the worms lie evermore.
    Ill I saw a dead corpse making a strange cry,
With dead feet planted on a high tombs floor;
The dead stand round, with faces that implore;
His dead hands bless them, stretched forth on high.
    THE GROTESQUES –And art thou God?–and art thou majesty?–And art thou he whom all the dead adore?–And art thou he that hath the skies in store?–Nay, nay, dead dust, dead dust, and vanity.
    And wouldst thou rise up to the lighted sky?–
Nay, nay, thy limbs are rotten on the floor;
Thou shalt not out from thy polluted sty;
    Thou wouldst become divinity once more,
Thou dreamest of splendour that shall never die;
And in thy heart the worms lie evermore.
    I saw a dead corpse lying on the floor
Of a tomb; worms were in its womans head,
Its black flesh lay about it shred on shred,
And the dead things slept in its bosom hoar.
    And evermore inside that loathed door,
It turnd itself as one upon a bed,
It turnd itself as one whom sleep hath fled,
As one that the sweet pangs of passion bore.
    THE GROTESQUES
    And from its passionate mouths corrupted sore, And from its lips that are no longer red, Came forth loves accents; and it spake, and said.

—The Pleiades and nights noon-hours are oer, And I am left alone in wearyhead. And in its heart the worms lie evermore.

DEAD DIALOGUE 1st Corpse. I would now that the sweet light of the sun Might once again shine down upon my face;

So weary am I of my rottenness. 2nd Corpse. Rejoice that now at least thou art done with life;

This thing shall nevermore return. 1st Corpse. At last
My body is aweary of the tomb;
It is a hundred years since in the grave
I have lain down between four narrow walls,
Shut up with putrid darkness and the worm.
There is no flesh upon my body now,
That was so long a-rotting; on my shelf
Here am I now nothing but stinking bones,
That have had life beneath the face of the sun.

DEAD DIALOGUE 3rd Corpse. / am not yet utterly putrified,
And the worms yet within my flesh abound; I do repent me that I did not learn What life was, while I livd beneath the sun–
At least then I might think of what I had done;
But I am rotten, and I have not livd. 1st Corpse. I would that I might leave this place of ordure
And look once more upon the face of the world,
Where the sun is. 2nd Corpse. O foolish ragged-bones,
Wouldst thou show forth thy dripping excrements,
And shredded rottenness to the face of day?–
Stink and be still, and leave us here in peace.

1st Corpse. Envy me not, O stench, slop-face, dung-eyes;
My bones are clean and dry as the tombs walls,
And stink not; as for thee, thou art a sink. DEAD DIALOGUE 2nd Corpse. Envy me not, thou, that I am so sweet

The black worms love me; hungry were that worm That on thee preys.

4th Corpse. Be silent, both ye dead and rotten things; Lo I, that was unburied yesterday, Am fair and smooth and firm, and almost sweet; If that I were not dead, one might me love. 3rd Corpse. Is it so sweet a thing, this love, this love? 2nd Corpse. Thy lips are green for kissing, and streaks of black Streak over thee where the worms have not yet been!

4th Corpse. Ha, ha, I know wherefore thou speakest so: Because thy torture is too great for thee, And the worms gnawing, and thy bodys rottenness, And the rottenness in thy bones and in thy brain!

1st Corpse. O beautiful, O dead, O spit upon,
He speaketh well that is but lately dead;
Thy flesh lies all along thee like green slime,
O pudding gravied in thine own dead sauce!

DEAD DIALOGUE 2nd Corpse. Rotten one!
1st Corpse. Dung-heap!

2nd Corpse. Dead one!
ist Corpse. Beast! beast! beast!
Therefore perhaps, thou art so early dead? 2nd Corpse. They say that those thou lovedst were not men, 0 goat-face–Shall I say what was thy death?
4th Corpse. Come, come, my brothers, be not so slanderous;
We have all been the same upon the earth. 3rd Corpse. Thou sayest true, new brother, 1st Corpse. Thou sayest true.
2nd Corpse. I shall not suffer anything any more; (Aside.) I have left all that; I am evermore re-leasd; 1 shall not struggle and suffer any more; This seemeth strange and very sweet to me;
And I shall grow accustomd to the worms. 5th Corpse. Rejoice not thou, that thou art fallen Into a pit where people leave their dung;
There is no reason here for any joy.

DEAD DIALOGUE

Sepulchre. Be silent, now, ye spindle-shanked dead! Ye will learn to be silent when yare here For a long time; ye always spout and roar, At first, before the time of rottenness; But so I suppose it must be,–yare not the first, And ye shall not be the last; so fast i the world, So eagerly they are begotten, and they die, And they are begotten again; just for this end
Hideously propagated evermore. A Voice above singing. Golden is the sunlight,
When the daylight closes,
Golden blow the roses
Ere the spring is old;
All thy hair is golden,
Falling long and lowly
Round thy bosom holy;
And thy heart is of fine gold!

FRAGMENTS

And since i understood not what so strong
Driveth all these at such exstatic pace,
I too went down and joined in the throng;
And many sitting in a lowly place I saw, where sense and vision darkness clogs,
With one flat-breasted wife with munched face
And bestial litter as of rats or hogs;
These are all they that eat and multiply
In the same manner with low apes and dogs;
Like these they live and like these they shall die.
–Pass thou from these, said then to me that voice,
And heed not thou the stinking of that sty.
Then saw I them that did with wine rejoice,
Crowning their heads with roses of the earth;
I too sat down and joined in that noise,
But askd me soon–Why do all these have mirth?
From these I past, weary of myrrh and wine.
Others apart whose spirits had more dearth

    Sat solitary as who would fain divine,
FRAGMENTS
Of seeing and of hearing ill content;
    With these I sat, half drunken with the vine,
And sick of visions that aye came and went;
But all the knowledge that their striving found
Was but one vision more than wine had sent;
    All these also shall moulder in the ground.
From these I past as from dead flesh and bones.
Then came I where the kings of earth sat crownd
    Neath purple canopies on golden thrones;
These offerd me part in that changeless state,
Until my soul wearied of brass and bronze.
    Others whose sweating nothing could abate
Kingdoms and cities build and overthrow,
Till my soul wonderd at the striving great
    Of all the puppets in that puppet-show: —Doth the string move them with such urgency, That all their limbs such strange grimaces show?
—These are all they that do, one made reply;
In all their actions never could I find
What they were doing these things for nor why.
    From these I past as from the deaf and blind,
And ever as I went the solemn brawl
Of all these mad and idiot howld behind.
    I came to those that ceased not to call
        The world unto them, shouting oer and oer;
FRAGMENTS
    My heart knew not why these so loudly bawl;
And some stood round with faces that implore,
Asking for peace; and ever those that gave
Did but like these delude themselves the more;
    But rottenness shall stop all these that rave.
Last, some there were that did with vanity
Toil ever with unwearied hands to save
    And to eternize all things great and high;
With these I stayd, till my heart questioned:
—What are the things thou doest here and why?
    Whereat all these became as persons dead.
Then I arose from among these the last,
And followd then whereer my footsteps led;
    And among them that reigned then I past,
And among them that ever fain would know,
And among them whose lot with wine was cast; I past the prophets and the puppet-show,

 And among them that joyd in marble and in song,
And all that Seven tird of long ago.
 And is this all the meaning of that throng,
This all, O heart, that wast of seeing fain,
But like a circle that still seemeth long
 Because it goeth round and round again?
Not in all these doth any reason hide
No more than in the words of the insane,
 FRAGMENTS
 There is no ground for sorrow; nor in pride
For pride; nor in them that in gladness sate;
Wherefore with none of these shall I abide. The sought is vanity; the seeking great
 Vanity; the not-seeking vanity;
For none of these change I my solemn state.
 Then since no one could answer unto me
The question, and since no one could me tell
The wherefore of this endless Vanity
 Of all the spirits that on earth did dwell,
I said–I go unto the Absolute;
He will perchance release me from this hell.
 Him that made noisy what before was mute
I found upon a heap of filthy dung
Low-sitting in the fashion of the brute.
 In strange grimaces still his face he wrung,
Up to the chin within that filth immerst,
Which still his busy hands about him flung.
 –Do thou those clothes wherein he is inhearst
Take off, said I to one, and do not shirk.
He did, while still that being howld and curst.
 FRAGMENTS
 For there so thick and muddy was the murk,
And he still bore of clothes so thick a weight,
I knew not well what thing therein did lurk.
 Three coverings then that one removed straight–
Omniscience, Omnipresence, Omnipotence,
From off the thing that in the ordure sate.
 Then did his truth show clear to every sense,
A filthy idiot so foul and low,
That decency the perfect tale prevents.
 And I–O thou–whose nakedness doth show
Like one not in the womb to fulness brought,
Why are all things that are; if thou dost know?
 Then he replied from out the ordure hot:
–Brahma, great Brahma, Everlasting, I!
And I–Not such reply my question sought.

Answer thou me! And he still made reply: —Brahma, great Brahma! repetition vain.
I asked again: and—Brahma! he did cry.
Then one thereby to me—Why art thou fain
Knowledge to have from It? It knows not, It;
Why seek for truth among the low insane?
Then he that did within the ordure sit
Out of the filth that lay about his feet
Such things as children make with little wit
Made, and then broke, and did the act repeat.
FRAGMENTS —I have made all the worlds, he gibbered;
And I his labour with these words did greet.—Why dost thou these things? why, O why? I said.
No word vouchsafd the mouth of him that stank,
But giggling sounds and idiot uttered. Then seated in that place of ordure rank,
With his two lips he made a cackling sound,
And back within the friendly ordure sank. Then I with a great sad and awful voice
Cried out—O thou that rottest in this sty,
O thou whose soul in ordure doth rejoice, What art thou doing these things for and why?
Then one to me—His bliss is not to know
The infiniteness of his own Vanity; Therefore the soul of him that stinketh so,
Because his sense is blind and deaf and mad
Forever, knoweth not eternal woe.
Lo from the first his soul no reason had;
He thinketh he himself is everything,
And nothing is but him! He is not sad. Ignorance, ignorance, shrouds him like a pall;
Therefore thus low upon the fetid floor
He sits, and knoweth naught outside his stall. And I—He maketh naught outside his store.
Why doth he this? and in this fetid tomb
FRAGMENTS
Sitteth he here in madness evermore? How long shall iron, awful, gnashing doom
Leave him thus naked old and idiot
Blind deaf and stinking, in the loathed gloom? How long shall This within the ordure squat?
How long shall This cease not to beck and nod?
How long shall This cease not to rot and rot? And he—This rottenness that seemeth God
More woe than this nor any other mode
Shall know not, till It ceaseth in the sod. And as a gnat, a viper, or a toad,
Because its nature is not infinite, It too shall perish in the worms abode; Till then It suppurateth in the night.
Then from the world I turnd my steps afar; I came there where the holy Trinity

And all the blessed saints in glory are, And did the beatific vision see,
And how those happy are that once did mourn;
But my heart said—All this is naught to me; Nor knew I why all these should be reborn.
FRAGMENTS
Where moon-facd houris wanton arms do fling
Round Mahmuds blessed, I past by in scorn, For my heart dreamd a deeper revelling.
Then came I to that banquet more divine
That Jayadeva and that Jami sing;
And the fair goblet filld full of the wine
Brought the cup-bearer clad with wantonness;
And there with the beloved and the vine My heart grew weary of that blessedness.
From life I past, finding no joy therein.
The vision and the vine and drunkenness Still like a circle ever closing in.
Then I departed to the final peace,
Sick of what is and shall be and hath been, Of Brahma, as the drop sinks in the seas: I past out from the bonds of thee-and-me,
Lost in that Infinite whose being is Glory in all things and reality;
But therein I that was not I, alas In that deliverance from me-and-thee Where all illusion fadeth like to grass,
Found naught that equalld my undimmd desire; —If that reality then real was, What is that real more than trodden mire?
Then from all being did my spirit pass,
FRAGMENTS
Sick of all being whether low or higher.
Out of that circle unto nothingness
I came, unto Nirvana, the far goal
Of many a holy saint, where visions cease;
But nothingness did not my heart console.
Ah not in nothingness is any peace,
Nor in peace any peace, nor in the whole,
Nor in the vine nor in the vision, nor
In being nor non-being, nor in all
That man hath dreamd of and hath anguisht for.
Nay not in joy nor the vine jovial,
Nor in the perfume of the lovd ones breath,
Nay nor in anything anywhere at all;
Nor in illusion; nor what sundereth
Illusion; in the sundering of that chain
There is no joy; and not alas in death
Find I that thing whereof my soul is fain.
All these things also are all vanity
No less than sun and stars that wax and wane
Forever in the everlasting sky.

ENVOI
AT THE END OF THE CENTURY
   Now I am come to the nadir at last, to the absolute sorrow,
   Now all the stars are gone out of my sky; Night everlasting is mine without hope or desire of the morrow,
   All my lifes hopes are gone tombwards to die. All my lifes glories lie perisht around me; and lo with great laughing
   Laugh I out loud, and I care not at all; Here with mine Anguish, my Sorrow, my Madness, my Grief, I sit quaffing Wine, in high state in my echoing hall. This is the last night I drink with you, maniac wassailers dreary!
   Lift up your goblets and drink ere I go! Lo, I am easily bord, I am easily tired and made weary; AT THE END OF THE CENTURY
   Now at the last I am weary of Woe. Lo, I that walk in the flower crown season of youth-fulness golden,
   Think ye that all things my gladness can slay? Sorrow is fitting for dotards and them that are loathsome and olden; 7 am as one that goes ever away.
   Lo, I laugh out at Grief, lo, I laugh in unending rejoicing, I that have nightshade entwind in my hair; Heart of me, what dost thou here in the wearisome darkness, revoicing
   Yesterdays stale and forgotten despair? Now it is midnight; but soon shall the wakening glory of morning
   Shine in the East, when the darkness is gone; Now in my spirit that sat for a time in the darkness of mourning
   Waketh in gladness the mystical dawn. New spring laugheth without–to thy heart it is calling! and oer thee
   Soon shall the banners of dawn be unfurld; Wait thou no longer, O heart, O heart that art strong, for before thee
   Lieth the pomp of the great high world!
AT THE END OF THE CENTURY
   Now it is midnight; my Anguish, my Mourning, my
   Sadness, my Sorrow,
   Crown you with nightshade, and once more with me Drink and make merry; farewell! I am here with you now; on the morrow Sail I over the mighty sea.
   Postlude
SONG OF INDIA
   Now at the last, Zulaikha, all my sorrows olden
Are farther off than Europe or than China seem,
And like an idle dream
   The North is faded far off in the distance golden;
And here with thee I sit in perfect peace enfolden
Beside the Ganges-stream.
   Full well I knew that neer those northern promontories
Could give to me the dream that did my soul desire;
For there my heart did tire;

For always me allurd the strangely whisperd stories Of skies that burn with more consuming languid glories, And suns of mightier fire.

I dreamd of heavier suns than burn in skies of ours, And heavier airs that through the long long evening swoon
    Under a larger moon,
    And heavier-scented gardens filld with stranger flowers, And tropic palms that wave through all the long long hours Of endless afternoon. SONG OF INDIA
    At last now from that northern dream am I awoken,
At last I am come home over the watery main;
Long long I sighd in vain;
Now under tropic palms I lie in peace unbroken,
And mine own land I see, beloved, and hear spoken
My natal tongue again.
    Zulaikha, past is all the longing and endeavour;
    The palm-trees sleep, and sleeping move not any leaf;
    Perisht is woe and grief;
    Stilly the padmas float upon the holy river;
    Among all these we two with languid eyes forever
    Lie sunk in endless kief.
    Before us riseth white our marble-builded palace;
Thou hast let fall from out thy hands that weary are
The volume of Attar.
    Thy hand hath spilld the wine within the silver chalice;
Upon the river winding through the distant valleys
Sleepeth the nenufar.
    From out the oleanders languid slumber steepeth,
And thou, Zulaihka, dost, in rest too deep for dream,
Like one enchanted seem;
    Thy beauty now in waking slumber sunken sleepeth,
    SONG OF INDIA
    And dreaming past thy wholly closed eyelids creepeth The sleepy-flowing stream.
    Thou hast the light of Asia in thy face divinest,
    And in thy scented mouth and in thy lotus-eyes,
    O wine of Paradise!
    O moon-facd love that by the sacred stream reclinest,
    Hath this world anything for which in vain thou pinest?
    That thing shall be thy prize.
    The caravans that in the desert, heavy-laden,
    By unknown oases pitch their sun-blackend tents,
    Shall bring thee all sweet scents
    Wherein delight in heaven the houris ever-maiden–
    Patchouli, nard, and myrrh, from many a distant aden
    Of heavenly indolence.
    All kinds of gems wherefore thine almond eyes have yearning, In heaps, wherein to bathe thy beauties languorous,

O maiden amorous,
They shall bring home to thee from distant isles returning–
Pearl, sapphire, diamond, topaz, and ruby burning,
And opal luminous.
SONG OF INDIA
Thou art that sweet whereof all poets dead have chaunted, Therefore my soul hath sought thy face oer pathless seas, Here to have endless peace;
Thou art the garden of delight with slumber haunted, Thy perfume maketh dream of desert lands enchaunted, And far-off oases.
Thou hast that beauty in thine all-consuming glances
That openeth the ways to far enchanted skies,
And in thy lotus-eyes
Thou hast the light that shineth in the countenances
Of them whose eyes have seen the glory which entrances
The blest of Paradise.
Thou art all sweets that unto perfect joy devote us, In thee all spices and all scents together come,
O lute that now art dumb!
Thou art musk, frankincense, amomum, stephanotis,
Thou art the fragrant wine, the paradisal lotus,
Thou art the opium.
Hashsheesh nor opium are worth not thy caresses,
Sweeter than opium to still the spirits drouth
Thine unassuaged mouth;
Him that hath known thy love no mortal grief distresses; SONG OF INDIA
Sweeter thy kisses are than incense which oppresses
The breezes of the South.
At last I am come home, come home; and all regretting Is with the North afar from thee and me away.
Behold O love, the day Is past, in Indian skies the holy sun is setting;
The muzin from his tower calleth unforgetting,
The faithful ones to pray.
Under the velvet night wide India reposes
Now in the scented dark the champak odours swoon;
Slowly the summer moon
Riseth into the azure night made drunk with roses;
And lo the camel-bells, now that the daylight closes,
Tinkle their quiet tune.
Behold, O well-beloved, neath the moonlight gleaming
The travellers depart from out the sleeping khan,
O perfume Asian!
And past the moonlit palace, where we two lie dreaming,
With camels and with horsemen like to shadows seeming
Departs the caravan.
SONG OF INDIA It is the starting hour, O most melancholy!

In long procession underneath the moons pale gleams,
Like something that but seems,
The caravan departeth to the desert slowly,
There far afar to seek through endless time the holy
Mirages of their dreams.

DEDICATION

These paltry rhymes, which loftier shall pursue
Than aught America of high or great
Hath seen since first began her world-wide state,
I dedicate, my brother, unto you.

ITE MISSA EST

Lightning Source UK Ltd.
Milton Keynes UK
UKOW040001190313

207851UK00003B/716/P